JOANNA MURRAY-SMITH

Joanna Murray-Smith's plays have been produced throughout Australia and all over the world, including *Honour* which had a public reading with Meryl Streep and was produced on Broadway in 1998, the National Theatre, London, in 2003, and in the West End in 2006. Other plays include *Ninety*, *Bombshells*, *Rapture*, *Nightfall*, *Redemption*, *Love Child*, *Atlanta*, *Flame* and *The Female of the Species*, many of which have been translated into other languages and adapted for radio. Her novels include *Truce* (1994), *Judgement Rock* (2002), both published by Penguin Australia, and *Sunnyside* (2005), also published in the United Kingdom by Viking. She lives near Melbourne with her husband and three children.

Other Titles in this Series

Howard Brenton
ANNE BOLEYN
BERLIN BERTIE
FAUST – PARTS ONE & TWO
    after Goethe
IN EXTREMIS
NEVER SO GOOD
PAUL
THE RAGGED TROUSERED
    PHILANTHROPISTS *after* Tressell

Alecky Blythe
CRUISING
THE GIRLFRIEND EXPERIENCE
LONDON ROAD

Caryl Churchill
BLUE HEART
CHURCHILL PLAYS: THREE
CHURCHILL: SHORTS
CLOUD NINE
A DREAM PLAY *after* Strindberg
DRUNK ENOUGH TO SAY
    I LOVE YOU?
FAR AWAY
HOTEL
ICECREAM
LIGHT SHINING IN
    BUCKINGHAMSHIRE
MAD FOREST
A NUMBER
SEVEN JEWISH CHILDREN
THE SKRIKER
THIS IS A CHAIR
THYESTES *after* Seneca
TRAPS

Ariel Dorfman
DEATH AND THE MAIDEN
PURGATORIO
READER
THE RESISTANCE TRILOGY
WIDOWS

Helen Edmundson
ANNA KARENINA *after* Tolstoy
THE CLEARING
CORAM BOY *after* Gavin
GONE TO EARTH *after* Webb
LIFE IS A DREAM *after* Calderón
THE MILL ON THE FLOSS *after* Eliot
MOTHER TERESA IS DEAD
WAR AND PEACE *after* Tolstoy

Stella Feehily
DREAMS OF VIOLENCE
DUCK
O GO MY MAN

Debbie Tucker Green
BORN BAD
DIRTY BUTTERFLY
RANDOM
STONING MARY
TRADE & GENERATIONS

Ayub Khan-Din
EAST IS EAST
LAST DANCE AT DUM DUM
NOTES ON FALLING LEAVES
RAFTA, RAFTA…

Tony Kushner
ANGELS IN AMERICA –
    PARTS ONE & TWO
CAROLINE, OR CHANGE
HOMEBODY/KABUL

Elizabeth Kuti
THE SIX-DAYS WORLD
THE SUGAR WIFE

Liz Lochhead
BLOOD AND ICE
DRACULA *after* Stoker
EDUCATING AGNES ('The School
    for Wives') *after* Molière
GOOD THINGS
MARY QUEEN OF SCOTS GOT HER
    HEAD CHOPPED OFF
MEDEA *after* Euripides
MISERYGUTS & TARTUFFE
    after Molière
PERFECT DAYS
THEBANS

Linda McLean
ANY GIVEN DAY
ONE GOOD BEATING
RIDDANCE
SHIMMER
STRANGERS, BABIES

Joanna Murray-Smith
BOMBSHELLS
THE FEMALE OF THE SPECIES

Diane Samuels
3 SISTERS ON HOPE STREET
    with Tracy-Ann Oberman
KINDERTRANSPORT
TRUE LIFE FICTION OF MATA HARI

Amanda Whittington
BE MY BABY
LADIES' DAY
LADIES DOWN UNDER
SATIN 'N' STEEL

Joanna Murray-Smith

HONOUR

NICK HERN BOOKS
London
www.nickhernbooks.co.uk

A Nick Hern Book

Honour first published in this revised edition in Great Britain as a paperback original in 2003 by Nick Hern Books Limited, 14 Larden Road, London W3 7ST by arrangement with Currency Press, Australia

Reprinted 2006, 2007, 2009, 2011

Honour originally published in Australia in 1995, revised in 1997

Honour copyright © 1995, 1997, 2003 Joanna Murray-Smith

Joanna Murray-Smith has asserted her right to be identified as the author of this work

Cover image: Getty Images

Typeset by Country Setting, Kingsdown, Kent
Printed and bound in Great Britain by CPI Antony Rowe, Chippenham, Wiltshire

A CIP catalogue record for this book is available from the British Library

ISBN 978 1 85459 728 1

Acknowledgements

Thanks to Carrillo Gantner, and to Aubrey Mellor and
Jill Smith and all at Playbox, as well as to Katharine Brisbane,
Victoria Chance and Currency Press. Thanks also to Ariette
Taylor, Julia Blake, John Gregg, Natasha Herbert and Belinda
McClory, who taught me so much about this play. Thanks also
go to Edward Napier, John Patrick Shanley, Leslie Urdang,
Peter Manning and Ron Kastner.

For this British version of the play, particular thanks go to
Roger Michell. I am also grateful to Matthew Byam Shaw, the
Royal National Theatre and, as always, to Sarah Jane Leigh.

My thanks also go to Raymond Gill for husbanding and
fathering so generously while this play was being written.

Honour received its British premiere on 21 February 2003 in the Cottlesloe Theatre at the National Theatre. Press night was 27 February 2003. The cast was as follows:

HONOR	Eileen Atkins
GEORGE	Corin Redgrave
SOPHIE	Anna Maxwell Martin
CLAUDIA	Catherine McCormack

Director   Roger Michell
Designer   William Dudley
Lighting Designer   Rick Fisher

Honour was revived at the Wyndham's Theatre, London, on 14 February 2006 (previews from 7 February), with the following cast:

HONOR	Diana Rigg
GEORGE	Martin Jarvis
SOPHIE	Georgina Rich
CLAUDIA	Natascha McElhone

Director   David Grindley
Designer   Liz Ashcroft
Lighting Designer   Jason Taylor
Sound Designer   Gregory Clarke
Composer   Simon Slater

Honour was commissioned and first performed by the Playbox Theatre Centre, Melbourne, Australia, on 14 November 1995 with the following cast:

HONOR	Julia Blake
GEORGE	John Gregg
CLAUDIA	Natasha Herbert
SOPHIE	Belinda McClory

Director   Ariette Taylor
Designer   Trina Parker
Lighting Designer   Philip Lethlean
Original Music   Peter Crosbie

Honour was first produced on Broadway by Ron Kastner and Marcus Viscidi in association with New York Stage and Film at the Belasco Theatre in April 1998, with the following cast:

HONOR	Jane Alexander
GEORGE	Robert Foxworth
CLAUDIA	Laura Linney
SOPHIE	Enid Graham

Characters

HONOR, *a beautiful, elegant woman, around sixty.*

GEORGE, *Honor's husband. An attractive, youthful man, around sixty.*

SOPHIE, *their twenty-four-year-old daughter*

CLAUDIA, *a striking young woman around thirty*

Scene One

The stage is in darkness. Only GEORGE*'s voice can be heard.*

GEORGE. First and foremost, a communicator. (*Beat.*)
Unafraid to tackle the real issues. (*Beat.*) No. No. Always
ready to plumb the depths of social and political change, he
has – he has – convincingly merged an intellectual prowess
with literary – no with a literary, no – with a distinctive
literary style. No. No. (*Beat.*) An adventurer into the heartland of a nation's cultural – An adventurer into the cultural
heartland of a nation's – It's all a little too pith helmet –
Wait a minute – (*Beat.*) Award-winning – is that awful?
It's probably unprofessional *not* to mention the awards –
Bestowed with the odd literary gong – pretentiously casual –
Why not just say it? Recipient of *awards* too numerous to –
No – No – (*Beat.*) – All right. Okay. (*Confidently.*) George
Spencer has been the authoritative – the single most
res(pected) – George Spencer has been the incisive voice
of a – the British intellectual establishment has long
acknowledged – For twenty – no – for – Love him or hate
him – George Spencer, the fearlessly articulate – *Fuck*!
(*Beat.*) Look, this is awful – so, so – I *loathe* people who
talk about themselves in the third person –

Lights up. CLAUDIA *and* GEORGE *sit comfortably facing
one another.*

CLAUDIA. I asked you –

GEORGE. Yes –

CLAUDIA. I need your help. The introduction's –

GEORGE. Very tricky –

CLAUDIA. I need ideas –

GEORGE. Yes –

CLAUDIA. It's so hard to fit everything – to summarise a *life* in a couple of paragraphs!

GEORGE. It *is* an art.

CLAUDIA. I hope you don't mind –

GEORGE. Not at all – not at all –

CLAUDIA. It's very interesting –

GEORGE. Is it?

CLAUDIA. Oh, yes!

GEORGE. Because, you know – you know – a lifetime of interviewing can make one an intolerably longwinded interviewee – as if one finally allays one's sense of outrage at how much *more* interesting *oneself* is.

CLAUDIA. Not at all.

GEORGE. As an interviewer, one waits interminably for the question that never comes: What About You, Then? So you see, now I'm on the *other* side – I have a vast impulse to bore.

CLAUDIA. Well, your impulse is failing you –

GEORGE. I'm like some ancient explorer reminiscing – Tracing over rivulets of technique, remembering philosophical oceans –

CLAUDIA. But you're so *inspiring*! Some of the others were really, well, lethargic.

GEORGE. They were?

CLAUDIA. Yes. *Yes.* They were just these old men. These irrelevant old men.

GEORGE. And I'm not?

CLAUDIA. Last time we talked, I came away . . . *dazzled*.

GEORGE. Really?

CLAUDIA. Absolutely!

GEORGE. I know what you're doing, young lady –

CLAUDIA. No – Really –

GEORGE. Melting my defences –

CLAUDIA. Honestly –

GEORGE. So I 'open up'.

CLAUDIA. Well . . .

GEORGE. It's not a criticism . . .

CLAUDIA. Isn't it?

GEORGE. Not at all. I'm impressed. You have strategy.

CLAUDIA. I do?

GEORGE. And strategy is important. It's always important.

CLAUDIA. And is it working?

GEORGE (*laughing*). I think it might be . . .

Beat.

CLAUDIA. The truth is, I found that interview stuff very interesting. Especially since *I'm* interviewing *you*.

GEORGE. You know, a kind of vulgarity has insinuated itself into journalism via the television set. I always say an interview comes down to secrets . . .

CLAUDIA. Secrets?

GEORGE. One's life revolves around secrets. A good interview does not need to expose a secret. It simply reveals to us *why* a secret is fundamental to someone's life.

CLAUDIA. Fascinating!

GEORGE. Not really –

CLAUDIA. Yes – Yes!

GEORGE. What about you then?

They laugh.

What *about* you, then?

CLAUDIA. I'm nothing. I'm no-one.

GEORGE. How can you say that?

CLAUDIA. I've got no illusions.

GEORGE. If they chose you –

CLAUDIA. They saw in me a bright graduate with – with tenacity – and they knew I'd be flattered to do it so they needn't pay me much.

GEORGE. I'm sure you're too modest.

CLAUDIA. That's fine. That's really fine. Because it's true. I *am* flattered. And it will look good on my C.V.

GEORGE. The dreaded C.V.!

CLAUDIA. Middle-class girls are all the same. That's why we have to spend our whole lives singling ourselves out. The publishers are using me, but then – I'm using them.

GEORGE. Isn't that a little cynical?

CLAUDIA. Actually, an exploitative relationship is in many ways the most dependable relationship. I need them and they need me. No one's going to fuck anyone over.

Beat.

GEORGE. Do you have a title yet?

CLAUDIA. 'Movers and Shakers: Power and Influence in Modern Britain.' Pretty dry –

GEORGE. I like it!

They laugh.

Well, they wouldn't have wasted their time with someone who wasn't very talented.

Beat.

CLAUDIA. Thank you.

Beat.

GEORGE. You want to write?

CLAUDIA. Everyone wants to write!

GEORGE. Well, yes –

CLAUDIA. The truth is, I *do* write. Fiction. And I intend to become a very good writer. But I find it so pathetic – so indulgent to express that wish –

GEORGE. Well –

CLAUDIA. It's what one *does*, in the end.

GEORGE. Well, yes. But when you're young it's all ahead – it's *all* wishing. *Wishing* has the same currency that *doing* does in middle age.

CLAUDIA. We *all* intend. Only some of us achieve. I've always – oh no – this is *your* interview!

GEORGE. Go on . . .

CLAUDIA. I feel so comfortable talking to you. You really – You seem to –

GEORGE. I'm interested.

CLAUDIA. I've always been able to imagine things I want for myself and it's as if my imaginings are so perfect, so pedantic that reality just obliges them.

GEORGE. Like this –

CLAUDIA. Like this book.

GEORGE. And what else?

CLAUDIA. What else?

GEORGE. What else do you imagine having?

Beat.

CLAUDIA. Oh, that's secret . . .

Scene Two

GEORGE. And?

HONOR. I was with her in the kitchen –

GEORGE. I was with him in the garden –

HONOR. I was stunned –

GEORGE. I told him what a fool he was –

HONOR. She was drinking and she never drinks –

GEORGE. And?

HONOR. I thought perhaps – the children – But she said they were all right.

GEORGE. He didn't seem to care –

HONOR. She was beside herself –

GEORGE. He looked so fit!

HONOR. That's the thing –

GEORGE. I said: You do realise you're turning yourself into a pathetic middle-aged male cliché –

HONOR. And?

GEORGE. He said: I realise my actions are very threatening to my friends.

HONOR. Doesn't the girl care what she's doing?

GEORGE. Biological clock. A thunderous tick in the ear – This is her last chance to dance –

HONOR. She *does* dance. She takes him to clubs and he's so old people think he's a performance artist.

GEORGE. He says he loves her –

HONOR. How easily love is invoked to lend dignity to shallowness.

GEORGE. He says he loves her –

HONOR. He loves how she makes him *feel.*

GEORGE. At a certain age, young women don't necessarily like to be seduced, but they like to be seen to be seductive.

HONOR. At a certain age, men don't necessarily enjoy fucking, but they like to be seen to be fucking. And at heart, Jim's always been a selfish prick and Gwen spent her life catering to his grandiose ego.

GEORGE. What is it about facing death that makes a man turn to a tanning salon?

HONOR. Gwen said he bought himself and the girl His and Her Cartier watches.

GEORGE. He said he wants to sell everything and buy a yacht –

HONOR. He just came home and said that was it –

GEORGE. He'll wake up to himself –

HONOR. He'll wake up to a luscious thirty-five year old. History free. Cellulite free.

GEORGE. And when she starts talking babies?

HONOR. He'll see it as his chance to rewrite himself as a father. Because the first time around he was too busy making money.

GEORGE. He's sixty-three years old!

HONOR. This time around he'll be investigating the safest change-tables!

GEORGE. I told him: 'You've got one of the most intelligent beguiling women of our generation as a wife and I've got the other'–

HONOR. Darling –

GEORGE. 'Why do you want to trade a Bentley for a Toyota?'

HONOR. And?

GEORGE. He said: 'A Bentley belongs to a life I don't have any feeling left for.'

HONOR. It's so tragic –

GEORGE. It's so ugly –

Scene Three

HONOR. I'm afraid it's typical –

CLAUDIA. It's quite all right!

HONOR. He's trying everyone's patience –

CLAUDIA. I'm not worried –

HONOR. But that's George. He's probably stuck in traffic –

CLAUDIA. Actually, I'm glad to have this opportunity to talk to you.

HONOR. To me?

CLAUDIA. What better introduction to a subject than through the woman he has lived with for – for – thirty –

HONOR. Thirty two –

CLAUDIA. Years. My God! I can't imagine ever spending thirty-two years with anybody!

HONOR. We're very lucky.

CLAUDIA. Is it luck?

HONOR. Partly luck. Partly skill. Partly love.

CLAUDIA. Is it a natural state then, do you think?

HONOR. It's *my* natural state. Although anyone will tell you, it isn't easy –

CLAUDIA. No!

HONOR. *He* hasn't been easy –

CLAUDIA. Is any man?

HONOR. But then I'm not an easy person, either.

CLAUDIA. You're a writer too . . .

HONOR. I suppose I still am.

CLAUDIA. You can't *retire* from being a writer – It's a state of being.

HONOR. Perhaps. A toughness. A watchfulness. As Graham Greene said: in every writer, a chip of ice!

CLAUDIA. But you've stayed together?

HONOR. You just have to stick it out through the hard times.

CLAUDIA. Like when he resigned from *The Times*?

Beat.

HONOR. There were times I argued with George over his stubborn idealism.

CLAUDIA. In retrospect –

HONOR. This is off the record –

CLAUDIA. Of course –

HONOR. For someone who prides themself on intellectual independence, editorial interference is worth putting yourself on the line for. I thought he put principles above pragmatism, but he was right.

CLAUDIA. So there were tensions . . .

HONOR. We had our darker moments but we stuck it out.

CLAUDIA. Many don't –

HONOR. I suppose they don't –

CLAUDIA. But you –

HONOR. Yes –

CLAUDIA. Why is that, do you think? What gave you the – the strength?

HONOR. The strength?

CLAUDIA. Diligence –

HONOR. I wouldn't call it –

CLAUDIA. Whatever we call that kind of perseverance.

Beat. This is shocking to HONOR.

HONOR. Well, because we – we *love* . . .

CLAUDIA. How do you know where the heart of a relationship lies? In the very best moments, in the ordinary moments, in the worst?

HONOR. In all of them – You know the worth of what you're in. You know how much misery is tolerable.

CLAUDIA. So misery is part of what we might all expect of love?

HONOR. Well, yes. Yes. I mean, that's what – that's what gives a relationship depth. That's what love is, actually. A very complex mixture of pain and pleasure –

CLAUDIA. And security –

HONOR. Security is very under-rated –

CLAUDIA. And sexual desire –

HONOR. Of course. Although, you know – at our age – sometimes you'd really rather read the last chapter of your Anne Tyler than handcuff each other to the bed head.

CLAUDIA. She's that good, is she?

HONOR. Well – well, it's a joke! A joke! (*Beat.*) It has its underpinning of truth. This is off the record, of course –

CLAUDIA. Of course –

HONOR. A physical relationship is very, very important – but at a certain age – it can become a presence which is partly memory –

CLAUDIA. Memory?

HONOR. Well, one *remembers* what one has shared and that has a vigilant kind of life in the present.

CLAUDIA. That's – that's upsetting –

HONOR. Oh no! Not at all. I mean you still have a physical life together – of course – very satisfying – but passion – well passion is partly knowing who each other *used* to be.
I remember those first years with George and that contributes to my love of him now. Perhaps we exploit the past for what the present lacks. You know, it's a mistake to think that love belongs only to the present. It's incremental.

CLAUDIA. Fascinating . . .

HONOR. I must be boring you –

CLAUDIA. Not at all. Being so close to George – you're a great ally for this profile.

HONOR. Well, one could say, I see less. Perhaps there is less clarity.

CLAUDIA. I'm not sure I understand –

HONOR. One may become insensitive to character by being so – so exposed to it. Perhaps I see George *less* well!

CLAUDIA. Are you saying intimacy *clouds* knowledge?

HONOR. I don't know. I'd like to think we were still capable of surprising one another.

CLAUDIA. What an interesting – Most married women wouldn't say that – Most women in your –

HONOR. Middle-aged, you mean?

CLAUDIA. Well –

HONOR. Middle-class?

CLAUDIA. I'm trying to make a point here, not be, not be –

HONOR. I'm very happy to be middle-aged and middle-class! Only the young middle class find that derogatory – as if ordinariness were the greatest terror.

CLAUDIA. Do you like being a writer?

HONOR (*beat*). Yes. Yes. It's – it's tiring. It's tiring always leaving yourself – so – well, unless you're prepared to *feel* things – to feel things – there isn't much point. Which means that life is constantly upsetting. Even a middle-aged, middle-class life.

CLAUDIA. Do you see your relationship with George in political terms?

HONOR. Political? What does that mean?

CLAUDIA. Aren't there inherent consequences to the power dynamic in a relationship?

HONOR. Oh My Goodness, I've been awfully remiss at track-ing the 'power dynamic'. I'm afraid I just see marriage as how two people grow old together – it's a necessary loyalty.

CLAUDIA. Isn't loyalty just resistance to change?

HONOR. I hope not.

CLAUDIA. I think – if you'll excuse me – that women of your generation tend to be more generous about their husbands.

HONOR. Time is perhaps what makes one more forgiving –

CLAUDIA. I'm not sure I buy that –

HONOR. My dear, I'm not selling it. And the young are always unforgiving. That's part of your charm.

CLAUDIA. I think many women want to justify their choice to live through their husbands –

HONOR. Do you think I live through my –

CLAUDIA. I'm just saying some women use loyalty as a way of justifying their own absence of self. They need to say that all the sacrifices were for a point. *It* was worth it. *He* was worth it.

HONOR. That's rather patronising.

CLAUDIA. We're all victims of our contexts, aren't we?

HONOR. Victim. I hardly think so. I don't think I'm rational-ising my – my 'sacrifices'. What are those sacrifices?

CLAUDIA. Well . . . No, no you're right – It's very impertinent –

HONOR. I'm interested. Please – what do you see those sacrifices to be?

CLAUDIA. Well . . . Well, you were writing before your marriage weren't you? *Maiden Voyage* was published in 1973?

HONOR. I'm impressed –

CLAUDIA. It was – well, it won all the prizes, didn't it? It wooed a whole new generation to poetry.

HONOR. Thank you. It was published two years after we were married.

CLAUDIA. And then you got pregnant?

HONOR. Eventually.

CLAUDIA. And didn't you go to Stanford with George when he got the doctorate scholarship?

HONOR. Yes, for three years.

CLAUDIA. So you were following where he led?

HONOR. I was married to him!

CLAUDIA. Yes, but being, ah – objective – it was *his* career that was setting the agenda? (*Beat.*) These days, we have an awareness of what we give up.

HONOR. You mean, a resentment? Don't you think love gets suffocated in resentment?

CLAUDIA. I think love gets suffocated in inequality.

HONOR. If you love someone, you want them to flourish. Their success is your success –

CLAUDIA. So you *do* live through them?

HONOR. It doesn't matter if it's the man or the woman who steps aside to let the other succeed – it's *love* –

CLAUDIA. Ah yes, but it always *is* the woman, isn't it?

Beat.

HONOR. I could be fooling myself, but I always thought I enjoyed considerable status in George's eyes. By being a good mother. That he saw that as a remarkable achievement. And that – well Sophie – Sophie is more than – more than – a Booker prize. More than a top ten in the *Times Literary Supplement*.

CLAUDIA. Perhaps. But I don't think I could put my life on hold for the man I loved.

HONOR. Is my life on hold?

CLAUDIA. Only you know that.

GEORGE *enters.*

GEORGE. Darling –

HONOR. Darling –

GEORGE. Sorry, Claudia –

CLAUDIA. No – we've been having a very –

HONOR. Animated!

CLAUDIA. Discussion. Your wife has expertly made me look very foolish –

HONOR. I didn't intend –

CLAUDIA. You're absolutely – *Right.*

Scene Four

HONOR. She's a clever young thing.

GEORGE. At least they didn't send me some nitwit who doesn't understand the meaning of the word 'research'.

HONOR. The last one –

GEORGE. Asked me if this country really *needed* any more intellectuals –

HONOR. Oh dear –

GEORGE. So I said: 'Once we identify the smart gene, we might be able to eradicate it' –

HONOR. Whereas this one was –

GEORGE. Yes, she was –

HONOR. Even so, you could refuse.

GEORGE. Honor – I need the fifteen minutes –

HONOR. Darling, you don't –

GEORGE. Things are shaky –

HONOR. You've been saying that for –

GEORGE. What happened to the great editors? The men of vision? – If Harry drops the column, it's a *sign* –

HONOR. You're being melodramatic –

GEORGE. They'll bring in some thirty year old who peppers his insights with references to deconstructionism and the Brady Bunch.

HONOR. There are other possibilities – *The Observer* – *The Sunday Times*.

GEORGE. They're run by *managers*, Honor. They don't want intellectuals. They want clairvoyants and food writers. It's all about really good risotto.

HONOR. You're so cynical at the moment.

GEORGE. I *like* to be cynical. Cynical is lovely. It's jauntier than hopeful.

HONOR. I love you.

GEORGE. I love you.

HONOR. She reminded me of – she –

GEORGE. Who?

HONOR. The girl. Woman. Claudia.

GEORGE. Claudia?

HONOR. Yes. Reminded me of – of *me* . . .

GEORGE. When?

HONOR. Well, not me exactly. But me without – without good fortune.

GEORGE. You mean –

HONOR. She's a clever thing –

GEORGE. Very focussed, for that age, very – I wish Sophie had a bit of her – She's tenacious.

HONOR. And she's beautiful.

GEORGE. Is she?

HONOR. She has something of my early ambition. And she's very bright. Yet she has this – toughness – as if she's afraid of being damaged –

GEORGE. Maybe she *has* been damaged –

HONOR. As if somehow, she wasn't quite –

GEORGE. Always composing histories – the writer's compulsion . . .

HONOR. *Loved.* Maybe she was loved in every identifiable way, ballet lessons, party shoes, good schools, but not –

GEORGE. Can we not – ?

HONOR. Perhaps her mother just felt some tremor of loss in mothering that made her – stand back from –

GEORGE. Claudia.

HONOR. Anyway. She'll go far. She's driven. And she'll – she'll – life will soften her up eventually.

GEORGE. Well, try not to dissect her – that way that you do. Your habitual inquisition –

HONOR. My inquisition?

GEORGE. That way that you do. Dragging things out. She's – she's vulnerable, I think . . .

HONOR. You're the journalist, my love – the one who finds truth more compelling than kindness.

GEORGE (*playful*). Journalists are far superior, morally, to writers.

HONOR. Oh, really?

GEORGE. We wear our appetites out there. You ask your casual little questions and then – years later, a book appears – unattributed, devastating.

HONOR. Perhaps we're both guilty of liking words more than people.

GEORGE. I hope you didn't run that one by Claudia with the tape running –

HONOR. No, I deftly fielded her questions about you.

GEORGE. *What* about me?

HONOR. Just how much of a sensitive, caring person *you* are.

GEORGE. And did *you* find the truth more compelling than kindness?

HONOR. No, actually. I painted a very nice portrait of you. Very large in the feminine side.

GEORGE. Good.

HONOR. She thought I was defending you as a way of defending my life with you –

GEORGE. And?

HONOR. I denied it. And yet, I sort of – just neatly avoided the less impressive things about you. Now why?

GEORGE. Like what?

HONOR. Why would I protect you if not to protect myself?

GEORGE. Because you love me.

HONOR. Well, yes because I *do* love you. But I wonder if something in me was embarrassed to say those things – those things that make me look –

GEORGE. What?

HONOR. Like a victim.

GEORGE. What!

HONOR. Just that.

GEORGE. How?

HONOR. You taking priority.

GEORGE. When?

HONOR. The early years.

GEORGE. You were happy for that!

HONOR. Yes –

GEORGE. I didn't impose that on you. *We* chose it.

HONOR. Sort of.

GEORGE. You *wanted* me to do the doctorate. You *wanted* me to write the first book. We had Sophie!

HONOR. Yes. But she made me feel a bit guilty about it.

GEORGE. For what?

HONOR. For the me that might have been, I suppose. I think she was rather disgusted that I hadn't propelled myself forward with the same velocity as you.

GEORGE. She's young –

HONOR. She's smart. (*Beat.*) You fell in love with 'The Writer', didn't you? Be honest.

GEORGE. That's who you were. Yes, I loved your – your talent.

HONOR. And I'm not 'The Writer' any more.

GEORGE. You write!

HONOR. Come on, George!

GEORGE. But that's youth! To fall in love with all that we *might* become.

HONOR. Is that only youth?

GEORGE. Yes.

HONOR. Well, I never quite became what I might have, did I?

Beat.

I wonder . . .

GEORGE. What?

HONOR. Whether you haven't encouraged me to lose the one thing you actually value most.

GEORGE. Which is?

HONOR. Glory.

GEORGE. Why would that mean anything to me? Over Sophie. Over love?

HONOR. Because if I'm glorious and I choose you, you're glorious too.

Scene Five

CLAUDIA. They like it a lot.

GEORGE. Good!

CLAUDIA. They said the questions were savvy enough to draw out your erudition and complexity –

GEORGE. It doesn't take much to draw them out!

CLAUDIA. Only they want me to round out the more personal side –

GEORGE. What makes George Spencer tick.

CLAUDIA. I said to my editor that I wasn't going to subject you to that –

GEORGE. But my dear, that's your job –

CLAUDIA. I'll drag the others into the mire of their divorces and breakdowns if that's what they want, but I'm not going to do it to you.

GEORGE. That's kind, but –

CLAUDIA. I like you.

Beat.

GEORGE. That makes me happy.

Beat.

CLAUDIA. Besides which, what is there to tell? You have a daughter at Cambridge, right?

GEORGE. Right.

CLAUDIA. And a wife who loves you, right?

GEORGE. Yes.

CLAUDIA. And a beautiful house in North London, with affectionately dedicated volumes from Gore Vidal, Julian Barnes, ecetera, etcetera?

GEORGE. Yes!

CLAUDIA. So excuse me for saying so, but who is going to find that riveting?

GEORGE (*uncomfortable*). Ah, exactly.

CLAUDIA. It's just one more bourgeois fairytale. Not to denigrate you, or anything –

GEORGE. Not at all.

CLAUDIA. Am I being unfair?

GEORGE. A very big part of journalism is about denying the stereotype. The more you categorise, the blander the story. Every life has its tragedies –

CLAUDIA. Like the day Tina Brown took over the *New Yorker*?

GEORGE *laughs uncomfortably.*

GEORGE. We all nurse our grudges, our losses, our
compromises –

CLAUDIA. Your compromises?

GEORGE. Of course. I'm not just George Spencer, the public
figure. There are so many contradictions within a person –

CLAUDIA. Such as?

GEORGE. The generous and the venal. The controlled and
the – the carnal. Who are we beneath who we appear to be?

Beat.

CLAUDIA. You tell me.

GEORGE. Well no, my dear. *You* tell *them.*

CLAUDIA. Then help me. Help me to understand.

GEORGE (*slowly*). Sometimes one craves something for
years – for years – and one just defers from – from acting
on it . . .

CLAUDIA. Why?

GEORGE. Because it might not be the best or noblest thing.

CLAUDIA. You're telling me you've experienced anguish?

GEORGE. Of course I have.

CLAUDIA. Like me? With all my wishing to be something
I'm not?

GEORGE. You're young. You have the chance to explore all
your callings –

CLAUDIA. Which are no doubt delusions –

GEORGE. Not so. My God – you're so – you're so bright –
and, and – attractive –

CLAUDIA. Do you think so?

GEORGE. Yes!

CLAUDIA. Really?

GEORGE. My God, yes! But people must tell you that all
the – a gi – woman like you, you must have lots of – of
admirers –

CLAUDIA. But they're fools – I know I'm desirable. I've
known that since I was twelve. There's something about me
that makes men want to fuck me.

Beat.

GEORGE. Aha –

CLAUDIA. But big deal! *That's* not the measure of a woman's
self-confidence any more, is it?

GEORGE. Oh, no, no!

CLAUDIA. I know I'm clever. I've been thrown into situations
with very, very intelligent people. Writers and politicians
and I've held my own. I've listened to myself and while I'm
having this conversation with them, there's a part of me
saying: 'Claudia, you know how to do this. You're coming
across as thoroughly convincing'.

GEORGE. I'm sure you do –

CLAUDIA. And there's this little flash of understanding in
those moments, that *this* is what I've got. A persuasiveness.

GEORGE. Yes, I can imagine –

CLAUDIA. And I experience this high, this incredible *rush* –

GEORGE. Right!

CLAUDIA. Like – Like when you're in bed with someone and
you're naked and you feel how glorious your own body is
and how it's just sending the person you're with wild with
desire and – and – you're touched – in that perfect way and
you rise up, and your blood is just pumping, pumping until
you just *explode* –

GEORGE (*deeply affected*). Yes!

CLAUDIA. With joy –

GEORGE (*embarrassed*). Right . . .

CLAUDIA. But being able to satisfy those standards of – of what? Intellectual camaraderie? What then? You just think, what else is there? What else is there?

GEORGE. My dear girl, you give yourself such a hard time!

CLAUDIA. I do?

GEORGE. Whether men want to – to – whether or not you're sexually attractive has nothing to do with the fact that you are also exceptionally bright and very determined and I doubt there is anything you couldn't do if you felt passionate about it.

CLAUDIA. Really?

GEORGE. Yes!

CLAUDIA. So you find me intellectually – competent?

GEORGE. You have a ravishing mind.

CLAUDIA. You don't think my ambitions are naive then?

GEORGE. There's a quality to your intellect that shines.

CLAUDIA. But do I have – is there anything *original* about me?

GEORGE. Your way of seeing things is exquisitely idiosyncratic!

CLAUDIA. So you don't want to fuck me?

GEORGE. Well – well –

CLAUDIA. I *am* passionate.

GEORGE. That's a lovely thing – Don't lose that – Don't lose that!

CLAUDIA. I don't intend to.

Scene Six

GEORGE. Honor –

HONOR. Yes –

GEORGE. Honor –

*She looks at him. She knows immediately something
profoundly strange has happened.*

HONOR. Are you ill?

GEORGE. No –

HONOR. Sophie –

GEORGE. No – no.

*She waits. She can't imagine what could be so terrible, if
her two loved ones are all right.*

Honor, I – I . . .

Beat.

We have to talk.

She waits.

I'm leaving.

HONOR. You're leaving?

GEORGE. Yes.

Beat.

HONOR. Where are you leaving for?

GEORGE. I don't know.

HONOR. What?

GEORGE. I'm – I'm leaving you.

HONOR. What?

GEORGE. Yes.

Beat.

HONOR. You're leaving me?

GEORGE. Yes.

HONOR. Say it again.

GEORGE. I'm leaving.

HONOR. This. This. Our.

GEORGE. Yes.

Beat.

HONOR. Just like this?

GEORGE. I don't know how –

HONOR. Just like this?

GEORGE. I – I don't know how –

HONOR. Today? Today?

GEORGE. I can wait. I can stay tonight.

HONOR. Why?

GEORGE. I'm – I'm. Honor. Honor. I'm not. I can't stay.

HONOR. You're leaving. Did you say that?

GEORGE. Yes.

HONOR. You're leaving me?

GEORGE. Yes.

HONOR. What's happening? What's happening?

GEORGE. I'm not – I'm not happy.

HONOR. You're not happy?

GEORGE. No.

HONOR. For how long? For how long haven't you been happy?

GEORGE. For a long time.

HONOR. Why didn't you? Say?

GEORGE. I – I couldn't.

HONOR. But this is us.

GEORGE. I didn't. I only realised how, how unhappy I've been – I only put it together. It's – I woke up to it –

HONOR. This morning? This morning you woke up to realise you don't want to be with me?

GEORGE. I've been thinking about it for – for months. For months. And it's come to the point where I – Where I – (*Becoming angry.*) Where I Just Can't Be Here Anymore.

HONOR. You're angry?

GEORGE. In a way, I am.

HONOR. You're angry with me?

GEORGE. No. No, but. But I can't – I can't – I can't describe it!

HONOR. What?

GEORGE. It's – It's – It's a feeling. It's a feeling, for God's sake. I – I love you but – but I – I don't want this any more. I don't want this.

HONOR. Did you say you are leaving me?

Beat.

Did you say you are leaving me?

Beat.

GEORGE. I can't. I can't. I don't want this.

HONOR. What?

GEORGE. This! This! I can't – I can't – I feel as if – I can't be my best self.

HONOR. What?

GEORGE. I've got these – I feel these huge, huge needs – these needs – and it's – it's just not possible.

HONOR. What needs? Tell me. Tell me! I'll help! I'll – I'll –

GEORGE. No! It's not. It's no. It's no good, Honor. It's no good . . .

Long silence.

HONOR. You love me?

GEORGE. Yes.

HONOR. You love me?

GEORGE. Yes – Yes, I –

HONOR. Then there's no problem. If you love me, there's no problem. We can –

GEORGE. Not like that.

HONOR. Like what?

GEORGE. I don't. I don't . . .

HONOR. What? Say it!

GEORGE. Love you like –

HONOR. You don't?

GEORGE. No.

Beat.

HONOR. You don't love me like a wife?

Beat.

GEORGE. That's *how* I love you. I love you like a wife.

Beat.

HONOR. Isn't that a good thing?

GEORGE. I don't want that kind – I don't want – I want a different kind of – I don't want a wife.

HONOR. This is. This is mad!

GEORGE. Honor –

HONOR. You don't want a wife?

GEORGE. Listen – I can't –

HONOR. You don't want a wife?

GEORGE. No. All right? No. All right? I don't want a wife.
All right? I Don't Want a Wife.

Beat.

HONOR. You love me?

GEORGE. I'll always love you.

HONOR. Like a – Like a, what? Like an old job? Like a pet?

GEORGE. I don't want. I specifically didn't want – to make
this. I don't want to make this degrading for either of us.

HONOR (*disbelieving*). What?

GEORGE. I think. I think I should go and we should, we
should just spend some time thinking and then – then we
can – discuss this civilly . . .

Silence.

Honor. I do. I do love you. I think – you've been – We've
had a wonderful life together. We've had. We've had
wonderful times. But I feel as if I – as if I'm dying – and,
and – I'm not ready to die yet. I'm not ready to die yet.

HONOR. What a shame.

Beat. Dawning on her:

Is there . . . Is there . . . ?

GEORGE. No –

HONOR. Someone?

GEORGE. No.

HONOR. Tell me!

GEORGE. No. No. It's not about someone else.

HONOR. Tell me! Please, George! Please George! Please, I
beg of you – don't let me – don't let me –

GEORGE. I am – I am –

HONOR. Don't let me *hear*!

GEORGE. There is – there is. I don't know. I don't know. I don't know that there's anything to speak of –

HONOR. My God!

GEORGE. Nothing's happened! It's just. (*Beat.*) There is someone –

HONOR. There is?

GEORGE. Yes. But it's not. It's not about her. It's nothing about her. She may. She may account for – for –

HONOR. Nothing –

GEORGE. Yes –

HONOR. Who? Who?

GEORGE. No one that you. No one that you – that you know –

HONOR. Who is she?

GEORGE. It doesn't matter –

HONOR. *It does matter!*

GEORGE. She's –

Beat.

It could be anyone – I mean – *she* isn't what this is about.

HONOR *waits.*

Claudia –

HONOR. Claudia?

GEORGE. The – the journalist – the – the –

HONOR. The girl?

GEORGE. The woman –

HONOR. Who came to – who had dinner here?

GEORGE. Yes –

HONOR. Who's doing the profile?

GEORGE. Yes.

Beat.

HONOR. She's so – She's – So –

GEORGE. She's very mature –

HONOR. She's half your –

GEORGE. She's very sophisticated –

HONOR. She's not much older than Sophie –

GEORGE. She *is* older. She's a lot more mature!

HONOR. My God, George. Do you realise? Do you realise? Do you hear yourself?

GEORGE. Yes.

HONOR. You're ill!

GEORGE. I don't think so.

HONOR. You're ill. You're terribly ill.

GEORGE. Honor – Jesus – I wish – I wish – I –

HONOR (*quietly*). Go away now. Go away now.

Scene Seven

HONOR. Your father's left.

Beat.

What I mean to say is. Ah. Your father has left me.

SOPHIE. What?

HONOR. He's not. It seems. It seems he's not in love with me anymore.

SOPHIE. What?

HONOR. He's – ah – found someone else.

SOPHIE. He's found someone else?

HONOR. Yes.

SOPHIE. He's left you for someone else?

HONOR. Yes.

SOPHIE. Dad's left you for another woman?

HONOR. Yes.

Long silence.

SOPHIE. Who?

HONOR. Claudia.

SOPHIE. Claudia?

HONOR. Yes.

SOPHIE. Who's doing the profile for that book?

HONOR. Yes.

Silence.

SOPHIE. Isn't she? Isn't she? (*Beat.*) She's my age.

HONOR. She's twenty-eight.

Silence.

SOPHIE. That fucking bastard.

HONOR. Yes.

Silence.

SOPHIE (*incredulous*). He actually said that. That he was leaving?

HONOR. Yes.

SOPHIE. You're telling me he just came home and said he wanted out?

HONOR. That's what happened.

SOPHIE. When?

HONOR. Tuesday.

Silence.

SOPHIE. Well, were there signs?

HONOR. I don't know.

SOPHIE. There must have been – there must have been signs!

HONOR. I didn't see them.

SOPHIE. You must have – have blocked them –

HONOR. I saw no signs –

SOPHIE. You must have blocked them. There are *always* signs.

HONOR. I don't know. Does it matter?

SOPHIE. You have to be alert. You have to be so alert. You have to notice everything!

HONOR. We've been married thirty-two years.

SOPHIE. Because people don't realise the little codes they use to speak to each other –

HONOR. I don't care –

SOPHIE. You don't care –

HONOR. I don't care about codes.

Beat.

SOPHIE. How, then? How – Can you – I don't get it. On Tuesday, he – ?

HONOR. Tuesday. Night. He. He told me. He broke down. He isn't himself. Or is he? Is he himself?

SOPHIE. Well, is it unusual? Have I been completely stupid? Is this Dad? I mean is this what he does?

HONOR. No.

SOPHIE. No?

HONOR. Not what he does. I think.

SOPHIE. He said he's leaving you?

HONOR. I think this is a – I think this is a – a one shot kind of – I think he met her and –

SOPHIE. Well that's very important, isn't it?

HONOR. Is it?

SOPHIE. Isn't it? Is he in love with her or – or out of – out of love – you know, out of love with you?

Too painful to answer. Silence.

Oh Mum –

HONOR. No. No! It'll kill me if you do that. It'll kill me.

Silence.

She came here for dinner. I cooked her a very nice watercress soup and Delia's salmon I think we had. We had homemade florentines with coffee. I thought, young single woman and all that. Could probably do with a good meal. She had it.

SOPHIE. It's his crisis. It's his fucking belated mid-life crisis – It's his – What? What's he proving? That he can still fuck! Is that it?! That he can fuck girls! Why doesn't he get a fucking psychiatrist instead!

HONOR. He didn't mean to hurt you –

SOPHIE. I'm not hurt!

HONOR. You should talk to him. Maybe you're just seeing things from my view –

SOPHIE (*incredulous*). What?

HONOR. He didn't want – He doesn't know what he's doing –

SOPHIE. You're defending him!

HONOR. Well –

SOPHIE (*incredulous*). You're defending him?

HONOR. He's in love with her for Christ's sake.

SOPHIE. You're *explaining* him to me?

HONOR. He can't force himself to do the right thing.

SOPHIE. Yes he can! Yes he can! Lots do!

HONOR. He can't make himself love me!

Beat.

SOPHIE. And all this. All this – this here. You. All of it. Me. That. All the time. All of us. That's what? That's what? That's shit? That's nothing?

HONOR. I don't know.

SOPHIE. Jesus, Mum. (*Beat.*) You have to fight!

HONOR. Fight what?

SOPHIE. *Him.* Fight him.

HONOR. Why?

SOPHIE. You can't. You're just. Why are you like this?

HONOR. Like what?

SOPHIE. You're just *accepting* it.

HONOR. What choice do I have?

SOPHIE. You should be angry – You should – You should – You're just –

HONOR. What?

SOPHIE. It's so typical.

HONOR. What's typical?

SOPHIE. To be the – The – Martyr. To be the martyr. To just accept this as if – as if it's inevitable. As if it's deserved –

HONOR (*exasperated*). That's not fair! What can I do? You want me to cut all the arms off his sweaters? Or burn down this house? What good is it?

SOPHIE. That's so – that's so passive! That's *so passive.* That's –

HONOR. Don't talk me, Sophie. Don't talk to me –

SOPHIE. Where's he living? Where's he living? With her?

HONOR. I don't know.

SOPHIE. Well, what's going on? Is it temporary or what? Have you talked to him?

HONOR. Just that I'll stay here in the house for the moment. And we'll talk 'when we've both calmed down' in quotation marks.

SOPHIE. I'm going to talk to him.

HONOR. I just want – I'm not defending him, but – you should remember. He's always going to be your father. He can stop being my husband. Or her – lover. But he'll never not be your father. So don't –

SOPHIE. What?

HONOR. Don't –

SOPHIE. What?

HONOR. Don't *become* me, all right?

Scene Eight

GEORGE. I want to be honest with you.

SOPHIE. Oh, right! Oh, *right*. That's good of you. That's lovely. That's so – so *you*. That honesty. That's what we all respect about you. That's what will go down in the – in the *profiles* of you!

GEORGE. You're angry.

SOPHIE. Yes, I'm angry!

GEORGE. Look, Sophie –

SOPHIE. What the fuck are you going to say?

GEORGE. What?

SOPHIE. I'm interested. I'm interested in what you can *possibly* come up with.

GEORGE. You're an adult. Let's not get hysterical –

SOPHIE. Oh right, you get to dictate the whole lot. What you do. What you do. And then *how* people respond to you.

GEORGE. I'm not trying to dictate – I'm trying to talk with you like two adults –

SOPHIE. This is adult then?

GEORGE. I'm afraid it is.

SOPHIE. Is she a good fuck, then?

GEORGE. Sophie –

SOPHIE. I'm a good fuck! I'm a good fuck! I'm in my twenties!

GEORGE. Listen –

SOPHIE. You're pathetic –

GEORGE. I don't think there's any point –

SOPHIE. Look in the mirror. You're old.

GEORGE. I'm not dead yet.

SOPHIE. *You're an old man.*

GEORGE. Fine. I'm an old man.

Beat.

SOPHIE. I hate you –

GEORGE. Yes.

SOPHIE. *Both.* You made it seem – you made it all seem – you *loved* each other.

GEORGE. Yes, we did.

SOPHIE. You set it up. Love. Fidelity.

GEORGE. We had that.

SOPHIE. You had – You weren't like other – You had feelings for one another that did not depend on – on – on *sexiness* –

GEORGE. No.

SOPHIE. You loved . . .

GEORGE. What can I – ? Because something's over doesn't mean it didn't have – it didn't have authenticity once.

SOPHIE (*sadly*). What good is that?

GEORGE. I loved your mother. (*Beat.*) I still love her.

SOPHIE. Don't do that! Who cares for that kind of love? If you love someone you don't do that!

GEORGE. It's complicated!

SOPHIE. No it's not! If you love someone, you don't do that!

Beat.

GEORGE. I'm sorry.

SOPHIE. Already. Already. I miss you.

Beat.

GEORGE. Things change. I can't stop this. I can't stop it.

SOPHIE. Why not?

GEORGE. What do you mean?

SOPHIE. *Why* can't you stop it?

Beat.

GEORGE. Because – some things have a – have an inevitability to them. If you – if you feel something so deeply, you can't make it vanish.

SOPHIE (*at a loss*). Well . . . Well . . . Didn't you love *us* deeply?

Beat.

GEORGE. I don't love your mother that way any more.

SOPHIE. You used to be very big on duty, I remember. 'Moral responsibility' – you used to go on and on about it.

GEORGE. This is different.

SOPHIE. Is it?

GEORGE. You can't dictate feeling as if it's theory.

SOPHIE. Isn't this where one's principles *are* tested? Or are they just for the public life, Dad?

GEORGE (*dawning on him*). You're a hard little thing, aren't you?

SOPHIE. What happened? What happened to you?

GEORGE. Listen to me Sophie, you don't know about love –

SOPHIE. Oh, really –

GEORGE. Love alters. Once I felt – for Honor, I felt – but –

SOPHIE. What?

GEORGE. It's not the same.

SOPHIE (*quietly shocked*). You don't love her?

GEORGE. I *do* love her. Yes. Yes. I do love her – but it's not –

SOPHIE. What?

GEORGE (*struggling*). It's not –

SOPHIE. Say it!

GEORGE. *Passion.*

SOPHIE (*shocked*). What?

GEORGE. It *can't* be passion!

SOPHIE. Why not?

GEORGE. Because history –

SOPHIE. What?

GEORGE. History –

SOPHIE. History what?

GEORGE. Kills passion.

SOPHIE. History kills passion?

GEORGE. I think so.

SOPHIE. Why does that matter? You had it once. Once is enough!

GEORGE (*on a roll*). Passion is – that's where everything comes from. The will to work. The will to get up in the morning.

SOPHIE. Is passion love?

GEORGE. I – I –

SOPHIE. Is passion love?

GEORGE. I think so. I wake up in the morning and I feel – I feel purpose surging through me – because she – she – she *excites* me – she's *alive* to me – I can't live without passion.

SOPHIE. But you *have*, apparently –

GEORGE. Yes, I have. (*Beat.*) But I'm not going to live without it anymore. (*Beat.*) I didn't try to fall in love. Love happens.

SOPHIE. You *let* it happen.

GEORGE. I fell. I fell.

SOPHIE. It's not the falling into – it's the falling away *from* –

GEORGE. She's your mother. Of course you must defend her.

SOPHIE. Jesus – don't you see? It's not *her* I'm defending. I think she's – she's a fool! Her life at the mercy of your whims!

GEORGE. This is no whim.

SOPHIE. You're – you're *pathetic*. But she – She invited this!

GEORGE. Jesus!

SOPHIE. Don't you criticise me for being tough! *I* didn't leave her!

GEORGE. She 'invited' this! How? How?

SOPHIE. Look at her! Always in the wake of *your* actions, *your* feelings, *your* needs!

GEORGE. That's not –

SOPHIE. *She's been in service.* Lover! Wife! Housekeeper! Therapist! Whatever the great man fucking orders!

GEORGE. Why do you see love as slavery? What's so liberating about a career, for Christ's sake?

SOPHIE. Oh right. Coming from the careerist of all time – *You used her up*!

GEORGE. That's a lie!

SOPHIE. I'm not defending *her*. When I stand here telling you what – what a truly weak person you are – I'm fighting for *my* life. I'm fighting for *my* future. I'm talking to you not as my father but as my husband. I'm telling you that in forty years I won't be standing in the wake of your weakness. I won't be weeping over you.

Scene Nine

HONOR. She's half your age!

GEORGE. Oh, that's bullshit! She's old enough to love, to be loved.

HONOR. She's young enough to be manipulated!

GEORGE. How? How?

HONOR. Because, sadly, you're a hero to her!

GEORGE. I don't think so –

HONOR. Oh, wake up, George! That's *why* you're in love.

GEORGE. Is it so hard to imagine someone genuinely admiring me?

HONOR. Frankly, *yes*!

GEORGE. This is ridiculous! I'm not going to defend myself to you –

HONOR. Go on, *try*!

GEORGE. Don't be absurd –

HONOR. No, really. I insist! Give it your best shot!

GEORGE. What gives you the right to say my love for Claudia is a lesser thing?

HONOR. *Thirty-two fucking years.*

GEORGE. For Christ's sake, Honor, we're over!

HONOR. We're over?

GEORGE. We're over. Okay? Okay? We're over.

HONOR. You're telling me you're –

GEORGE. Yes!

HONOR. You're –

GEORGE. Yes, all right? I am!

HONOR. Love? Love then?

GEORGE. I don't know. (*Beat. Shifting down in gear.*) Look. It's not about her and me. It's about me.

HONOR. Just you?

GEORGE. To feel. To feel as if it isn't all decided. How one lives a day. Gets up. Goes on into it. So many years together – forces – forces ritual on us, forces sameness –

HONOR. *Sameness*?

GEORGE. How can it not? I speak and you respond. You speak and I respond. How inventive can we be after thirty years?

HONOR. I like the sameness.

GEORGE. I don't.

Beat.

HONOR. You need help.

GEORGE. I'm all right.

HONOR. No, *I'm* all right. In the end. In the end. Because I'm still attached to reality.

GEORGE. Honor –

HONOR (*very calm, very soothing, caring*). This is *very* common, George. *Very, very common.* I'll get the name of someone. Someone *smart*, you know?

GEORGE. What? A shrink?

HONOR. If you look at this calmly, you'll see, you'll see –

GEORGE. I don't need a shrink!

HONOR. How can you say that! How can you think you don't need help? Don't you think this merits some *thought*?

GEORGE. I *have* thought –

HONOR. Don't you think you should test it? To see if you're – if you're *sane*, for God's sake.

GEORGE. I'm sane! I'm very sane!

HONOR. Mad people always think they're sane!

GEORGE. Don't pass this off as some neurotic mid-life crisis – Don't patronise me!

HONOR. Don't patronise me?!

GEORGE. Yes! Don't fucking patronise me!

HONOR. Don't fucking *leave* me!

Long beat. Shift in gear, gentle.

Wasn't there some obligation for you to warn me? To say: 'Honor, things are changing. I feel danger'?

GEORGE. It was too late.

HONOR. Well, then – then, it's true. You don't love me.

GEORGE. In the end, don't we – don't we love – don't we love ourselves just that fraction more? Isn't it about how we feel, how love makes us feel? It's so sweet to love another. It fills me out as if, as if before I was not quite whole, as if my blood was thin, my breath shallow – (*Beat.*) – Our love lost its vibration. It became normal, lost itself.

HONOR (*desolate*). Lost itself?

GEORGE. I feel – I feel – In front of me is some –

HONOR. What! What!

GEORGE. Some glorious space of uncertainty –

HONOR. Uncertainty?

GEORGE. Things unfixed, unnamed – The sense that anything might –

HONOR. Anything –

GEORGE. Yes. Yes. Anything.

HONOR. That's what you see?

GEORGE. In her. Yes. That's what I see.

Beat. Sadness and resignation:

HONOR. Did I look after you?

GEORGE. Yes. You did.

HONOR. Was I concerned for your concerns?

GEORGE. Yes. You were.

HONOR. Did I read all you wrote and tell you where you faltered and where you were strong?

GEORGE. Yes.

HONOR. Did I comfort you in the bad times?

GEORGE. Yes.

HONOR. Did I *love* you?

GEORGE. You did.

Beat.

HONOR. Who do I look after now?

Scene Ten

CLAUDIA. I'm ashamed.

GEORGE. Don't be ashamed.

CLAUDIA. But I *am* ashamed.

GEORGE. You have plenty of time.

CLAUDIA. But it's so confusing – I've got these *gaps* everywhere. Can we go through the list then?

GEORGE. What's on the list?

CLAUDIA. The Cold War. (*Beat.*) I don't get it.

GEORGE. You don't get it.

CLAUDIA. And Derrida. And – and – Relativity.

GEORGE. Relativity.

CLAUDIA. I've tried, but I don't understand relativity.

GEORGE. I'm shaky on relativity myself.

CLAUDIA. Explain Foucault. What was the Krushchev Report?

GEORGE. Fuck Foucault!

CLAUDIA. George!

GEORGE. I've always wanted to say that.

CLAUDIA. I just need to know – how they fit in. And I'm shaky on Nietzsche.

GEORGE *laughs. He loves the way her lips curve around the name.*

GEORGE (*flirtatiously*). Who are you shaky on?

CLAUDIA. Nietzsche.

GEORGE. Once more –

CLAUDIA. *Nietzsche!*

GEORGE. Mmm . . .

She laughs.

CLAUDIA. I love you for this.

GEORGE. I love you for everything.

CLAUDIA (*suggestively*). Everything?

GEORGE. The full repertoire.

Beat. They smile.

I was thinking today – What's keeping us here? Why don't I just sell everything. Buy a yacht – and we can – just disappear.

CLAUDIA. Buy a yacht?

GEORGE. Get out of here – Roam the world – Just us –

CLAUDIA. But I don't – I don't want to buy a yacht.

GEORGE. We've got each other – what else do we want?

CLAUDIA. But your work –

GEORGE. Oh, bugger the work – I'm sick of the paper – I'm sick of the think-tanks and the press club speeches and –

CLAUDIA. But this is where – You're – You're *important*.

GEORGE. I don't need to be important any more.

CLAUDIA. I don't want to sail the world.

GEORGE (*indulgently*). Then we won't.

CLAUDIA. I want to be brilliant for you. I want to be brilliant *together*.

GEORGE (*loving*). Then we *will* be brilliant.

CLAUDIA. We're not going to – we're not getting into that just living for – for love thing, George – because it – Things just fall apart.

GEORGE. But nothing much matters to me, apart from you –

CLAUDIA. But I don't want that.

GEORGE. You *used* to want that – You said – let me be your – your sun, your moon.

CLAUDIA. Yes but now, *now* – we have that and – We *can't* stop impressing each other. That's – that's fatal. We must continue to make our – our marks.

GEORGE. Do I really need to keep making marks?

CLAUDIA. Yes, George. You do.

Beat. They contemplate each other.

GEORGE. Am I dreaming?

CLAUDIA. No.

GEORGE. Am I dreaming?

CLAUDIA. I'm real. I'm standing here.

GEORGE. Look at you! So perfect.

CLAUDIA (*gently*). I'm just – saying, George – if we're not – if we don't be our – our best selves – we're just one more old man with his young lover – we're just one more cliché.

GEORGE (*dryly*). How nice.

CLAUDIA. Your mind excites me, George. You've got a very sexy mind.

They kiss.

GEORGE. What would I do if this hadn't – Where would I be if I hadn't – (*Beat.*) My life just started.

Scene Eleven

HONOR. What does that mean?

CLAUDIA. What?

HONOR. How do you *know*?

CLAUDIA. How do I know? Who can put that into words?

HONOR. Well. Well. *I* can.

CLAUDIA. You think you can bully me into explaining myself?

HONOR. I want to understand. *How do you know you love him?*

CLAUDIA. I don't have to convince you –

HONOR. No. You don't. But I'm asking you.

CLAUDIA (*rising to her challenge*). When I'm with him, I feel –

HONOR. Go on –

CLAUDIA. I feel –

HONOR. Say it!

CLAUDIA. All right! All right! I'll say it. I feel as if . . . I'm capable of anything –

HONOR. Capable?

CLAUDIA. Yes! Of doing something. Of *being* something.

HONOR. You love how George makes you feel!

CLAUDIA. Yes! Yes! All right!

HONOR. That's not love!

CLAUDIA. That's love!

HONOR. That's child love! You feel *young* –

CLAUDIA. Yes, I feel young! I *am* young.

HONOR (*astonished*). *You think that's love?*

CLAUDIA. And I do the same for him! With me, he wants to *do* things – to do *great* things –

HONOR. So you invest him with greatness! My, if you'd come along a little earlier, he could have won a Nobel Prize.

CLAUDIA (*defensive*). I *facilitate* his greatness. Yes. Yes.
I *know* I do.

HONOR. The love of reciprocal flattery!

CLAUDIA. Well, at least it's reciprocal!

HONOR. What a brutal little thing you are . . .

CLAUDIA. I always considered you very dignified, Honor.
Dignity's your thing, isn't it? It's the older woman's
singular advantage. You don't want to lose that.

HONOR. What are you so frightened of?

CLAUDIA. Nothing. I'm not frightened of anything!

HONOR. You're terrified you might lose something . . . What?
Certainty? What happened to you?

CLAUDIA. What does that mean?

HONOR. What calamity happened to you that you must bring
calamity to others? What made you predatory?

CLAUDIA. I don't *need* to be predatory! Your husband has not
felt love – real, sexual love for you for years.

HONOR. That's not – Not –

CLAUDIA. You said yourself –

HONOR. I did *not*!

CLAUDIA. I have it on *tape*, Honor.

HONOR. That's right. You taped me! You taped me because I
was useful to you.

CLAUDIA. So what if I did?

HONOR. You have a genuine talent for pragmatism, don't you
Claudia?

CLAUDIA. What's talent *without* pragmatism? You ought to
be an expert on that. When are women like you going to
understand that men don't *desire* martyrs? They want
women who want things for themselves.

HONOR. I suppose you'll be putting George on your C.V.?

CLAUDIA. Well, he's certainly been on yours for long enough.

Beat.

HONOR. I never realised – How – How savage you were –

CLAUDIA. I like the truth. The truth is savage.

HONOR. You like this, don't you?

CLAUDIA. Like what?

HONOR. At first I just thought that you – you were in the – like George – in the grip of something – but you're not, are you?

CLAUDIA. I don't know what you're talking about.

HONOR. You really enjoy this, don't you? You like to be at the *centre* of things.

CLAUDIA. *You* asked *me* to come here –

HONOR. And you're certainly not going to forfeit your – your *significance*, are you Claudia?

CLAUDIA. The difference between us, Honor, is that I don't intend giving up *anything* for *anyone*.

HONOR. And that makes you feel very proud, doesn't it?

CLAUDIA. Why shouldn't it? (*Beat.*) Look at me. (*Beat.*) Look at all I might become. (*Beat.*) Wouldn't you wish that for yourself? (*Beat.*) You could have been a great writer, Honor. You could have been up there – if you'd been more like me.

HONOR. So I should admire you. Is that it?

CLAUDIA. Your husband and I may have fallen in love but – but you and I – are still, on some level, greater allies than – than – he and I.

HONOR. *We* are allies?

CLAUDIA. You're a passionate woman – I *know* that. And you have – you're a writer. All around us there are systems to keep us *unrealised*. (*Beat.*) 'Softly, we make a child while from the cliffs, my father's ashes rain down on us, soft as silk.'

HONOR. Don't *you* use *my* words.

CLAUDIA. You should never have lost that part of you.

HONOR. I still write!

CLAUDIA. You haven't published anything since 1973! All these years, didn't you sometimes wish that all that – that way of feeling and seeing had a place, had a chance? Didn't it wear away at you that lesser talents had their faces in the literary pages while you basted the racks of lamb and looked over George's work? That you never felt the – the warmth of – of being thought great by *others*?

Silence as HONOR *acknowledges the painful truth of this.*

If anyone can understand me, you should. I'm rectifying your sacrifices.

HONOR. You take my husband and you tell me you're on my side?

CLAUDIA. I didn't take him. He offered himself.

HONOR. One happy day your face will shift around on those pretty bones and fall from grace.

CLAUDIA. I take care of myself!

HONOR. Time takes care of all of us.

Scene Twelve

SOPHIE. I recognise you –

CLAUDIA. I left when you started –

SOPHIE. We overlapped. You got a starred first, I think, that year. Your dissertation – it was published, wasn't it?

CLAUDIA. I worked out the system. That's all. I never really embraced real knowledge – that is, unassociated with, with purpose or self-promotion. I sought to understand how the place operated and then chose to operate within it. Which is, of course, its own kind of knowledge.

SOPHIE. I see.

CLAUDIA. So I got a – a flurry of firsts. But I – I lost the ability to cry at *The Great Gatsby*.

SOPHIE. I have not been blessed with a – a flurry of firsts.

CLAUDIA. Then perhaps you are – you *are* learning something – you are feeling something.

Beat.

SOPHIE. Actually, I'm something of a disappointment. (*Beat.*) To my father. (*Beat.*) I used to see you with – you were always surrounded by lots of – I used to watch you –

CLAUDIA. People hung around –

SOPHIE. No, but guys –

CLAUDIA. Yes –

SOPHIE. Didn't you used to go out with – you know – the actor –

CLAUDIA. Yes –

SOPHIE. We all – in the first year, he was seen as – we adored him –

CLAUDIA. He was so self-indulgent –

SOPHIE. Right – (*Beat.*) Still. We adored him.

Beat.

CLAUDIA. Sophie, maybe you could just bite the bullet and *say* –

SOPHIE. What are you doing, Claudia?

Beat.

CLAUDIA. I'm in love with him.

SOPHIE. You're in love with him.

CLAUDIA. Yes.

SOPHIE. You feel – towards him you feel –

CLAUDIA. Passion.

SOPHIE. Passion, yes.

CLAUDIA. Yes.

SOPHIE. Right.

Beat.

I guess it's his mesmerising physique.

CLAUDIA. Look, Sophie – when I got involved with George – let me be straight with you – I fell in love with George, not with George and his wife and his daughter. All right? So while I agreed to meet you here today, I'm not looking for your *understanding*.

SOPHIE. How can you be so – so unfeeling?

CLAUDIA. Unfeeling? I feel! That's why we're here now. Because I *do* feel.

SOPHIE. She says as she destroys people's lives! You're so full of strategy – You're even proud of it!

CLAUDIA. Whose lives am I destroying?

SOPHIE. My mother's life!

CLAUDIA. Actually, I think I'm saving her life.

SOPHIE. What?

CLAUDIA. Sophie, you're twenty-four years old. You don't own your parents. You're going to have to face the fact that they don't belong to *your* needs.

SOPHIE. But they do belong to yours?

CLAUDIA. George has a right to be happy.

SOPHIE. And Honor has a duty to be unhappy?

CLAUDIA. Should he give up his life to spare her feelings?

SOPHIE. Should she give up her life to indulge his?

CLAUDIA. He needs to be loved –

SOPHIE. He *is* loved!

CLAUDIA. He's a passionate man! I *make* him passionate –

SOPHIE. I don't want –

CLAUDIA. Your father excites me!

SOPHIE. Oh, please!

CLAUDIA. I like the way he treats me in bed, sort of like –
    like a – young thing –

SOPHIE. I don't – I don't want –

CLAUDIA. Like something he covets –

SOPHIE. Stop!

CLAUDIA. And when he comes into me, I . . . *complete* him –

SOPHIE. Stop! Okay! I don't want –

CLAUDIA. What happens to Honor or George is not your
    problem. Is it? However much you want to feel things on
    their behalf, you never will. Because you don't really know
    who they are.

SOPHIE. I don't think I need a lecture about them, actually.
    I know them fairly well.

CLAUDIA. Well no. You don't. I know them better than you
    do.

SOPHIE. Oh, really.

CLAUDIA. I think I do.

SOPHIE. You've met my mother – ah – *once*?

CLAUDIA. Have you looked at the themes running through
    Honor's poetry?

SOPHIE. Well –

CLAUDIA. Have you even read it?

- Yes – Of course I have.

we ever know our parents? Don't you look at
aphs of them in the sixties, when your mother
ong and looked so – so – ravishing – don't you
...um and think: My God. My God. She's Not Who
She's Been Pretending to Be.

Silence.

Do you know what your father longs for or misses or regrets? Do you know about their loyalties to each other – Who needed less loving, who more?

SOPHIE. I know about my mother's loyalty.

CLAUDIA. Oh, come on. You're not – you're not that immature, really, are you? Not to know how many different kinds of loyalty there are and how two people seek love and how they deny it, the tiny shifts of power –

SOPHIE. No!

CLAUDIA. Do you even know how they came together? Who wooed who? And how they secretly despised –

SOPHIE. They didn't despise!

CLAUDIA. *All* lovers do! Some aspects of the other sending chills through them – that makes them wonder about other lives, lives not lived, lives not chosen that might have been – have been – *more* or *less* honourable.

SOPHIE. No!

CLAUDIA. You think I bewitched your father? (*Beat.*) He loves me.

Beat.

SOPHIE. Well, I suppose he might.

Beat.

You're so – you're so clear. You seem so clear about things. Whereas I'm – I'm so – I can never quite say what I'm – even to myself, I'm so inarticulate. (*Beat.*) Some nights I lie awake and I go over the things I've said. Confidently. The

things I've said confidently and they – they fall to pi
(*Beat.*) And where there were words there is now ju
this feeling of – of *impossibility*. That everything is – there's
no way through it – (*Beat.*) I used to feel that way when
I was very small. That same feeling. Not a childish feeling –
well, maybe. As if I was choking on – as if life was coming
down on me and I couldn't see my way through it. What
does a child who has everything suffer from? Who could
name it? I can't. I can't. (*Breaking.*) But it was a – a sort
of – I used to see it in my head as jungle. Around me.
Surrounding me. Some darkness growing, something –
organic, alive – and the only thing that kept me – kept me –
here – was the picture of Honor and of George. Silly.
(*Beat.*) Because I'm old now and I shouldn't remember that
anymore. Lying in bed and feeling that they were there:
outside the room in all their – their warmth, their – a kind
of charm to them. Maybe you're right and it was – not so
simple as it looked, but they gave such a strong sense of –
love for each other and inside that – *I* felt – *I* felt loved. And
since I've gotten older I don't feel – (*Weeping.*) I feel as if
all that – all the – everything that saved me has fallen from
me and you know, I'm not a child any more. No. I'm not a
kid any more. But I still feel – I need – I need . . . (*Beat.*) I
wish – I wish I was more – Like you. Like you.

Scene Thirteen

HONOR. You're telling me you're staying –

GEORGE. At – at Claudia's. For the moment.

HONOR. At Claudia's.

GEORGE. For the moment.

HONOR. I thought – I thought she was. She was –

GEORGE. I need to sleep somewhere, Honor.

HONOR. You're *living with her?*

GEORGE. It was the easiest thing – I don't want our friends
to feel –

HONOR. I thought she was – she was – beside the point.

GEORGE. She is beside the point – In a way, in a way she is –

HONOR. But you're staying there?

GEORGE. Look I'm there, all right? All right? Can we move on?

HONOR. Tuesday to Friday. Friday. From Tuesday. That's –
that's (*Counting on her fingers.*) Tuesday, Wednesday,
Thursday, Friday. Four days. Not bad. Not bad. Four days to
leave a life and take up another.

GEORGE. It didn't happen like that.

HONOR. It didn't happen *to you* like that. That's how it
happened to me. Before Tuesday, my life was familiar to
me. I lived it. I owned it. It was mine. On Tuesday, it gave
me up.

GEORGE. Honor –

HONOR. Just a look. Just that – that look. As if a face caught
in certain light says more than any voice could – I knew. It
was all there. The girl and her youth and her skin and her
sex and your days and your nights and the lies and the
moments travelling towards this moment – and even now.
Even now was in that look.

GEORGE. Things had been changing between us for a long
time.

HONOR. You hid change. You hid it from us both. You lived
it – In another house with another woman, like visiting a
dream.

GEORGE. Nothing was going on!

HONOR. Oh. Yes. It. Was. You lay next to me in bed and
contemplated when you would see her again. How you
could move towards her. You looked at me and thought of
her. You *said* nothing.

GEORGE. You must have noticed –

HONOR. You're not. You're – Despite what everyone is saying – you're actually *not* an idiot, George. You doubled your efforts to keep ordinariness alive. You were a good husband until Tuesday.

GEORGE. I thought – I thought on some level –

HONOR. On some level, you'd spare yourself the difficulty of saying – of speaking out loud.

GEORGE. I'm sorry –

HONOR. Friday you were at the book launch with her. There she was. Madeleine told me. Of course she did. Sweet *schadenfreude*. She said you tried not to look as if you belonged together, but you left minutes apart and with the kind of overdone tact that is totally novel-esque behaviour for new lovers attempting to be discreet. (*Beat.*) Tuesday to Friday.

GEORGE. That's not –

HONOR. I *had* been invited to the launch. As your wife of thirty-two years, I've been invited to close to three hundred launches. *It was in my diary.* But of course, I wasn't going to turn up – I was doing what humiliated women do. And there you were.

GEORGE. I had to go –

HONOR. With her, you had to go with her.

GEORGE. We can keep delaying and delaying these things, but what's the point? You're talking about *decorum*, Honor –

HONOR. *Yes, I'm talking about decorum*! Yes I fucking *am* talking about decorum! Courtesy is not nothing, George. It means something. It's kindness. It's decency –

GEORGE. We have to get on with our lives!

HONOR. Listen! Listen to him! One week! One week!

GEORGE. You're hysterical!

HONOR. Book launches are an excellent way to get on with our lives. You're right! You're right! Some brought brief-cases, umbrellas, wives. You brought a new life. Slipped it

in there, effortlessly. Effortlessly. Tuesday to Friday. One
woman for another. One short history for one long one.
One cunt for another too. And a glance here, a glance there.
The whispers. The sibilant wave that must have followed
you around the room. And it's done. A book launch. A life
launch. And next time – next time – (*Breaking.*) they'll
expect *her*. They'll say: I suppose George will be bringing:
(*Beat.*) Claudia. Claudia. And that plain expectation is really
the triumph, the successful passing of the baton. Done.

Beat.

GEORGE. Look, Honor. I don't want to – to make this any
harder. Let's sit down with Gerry and –

HONOR. With Gerry?

GEORGE. And just work things –

HONOR. With Gerry?

GEORGE. Yes with Gerry! Why not? Why not? That's
sensible. *We have to be sensible*, Honor.

HONOR. You want to bring Gerry into this?

GEORGE. That's what people *do*.

HONOR. A lawyer?

GEORGE. Yes.

HONOR. You think this is about the *law*, George?

GEORGE. *Everything*'s about the law, Honor. When you take
the sentiment away.

HONOR. And that's what we're doing. Stripping our life of its
flesh and getting down to the bare, bare bones of the law.

GEORGE. The law keeps us –

HONOR. Keeps us –

GEORGE. Safe. In the end, you'll be glad of the law, Honor.
Because it's, it's there to protect you.

HONOR. Oh, thank you!

GEORGE. I don't have to do this! I don't have to do this! I don't have to advise you of your rights! I'm doing this because I care about you.

HONOR. What does that mean?

GEORGE. We'll just divide – everything – I'm fine about that.

HONOR. Oh, you are?

GEORGE. Yes.

HONOR. Why *wouldn't* we divide everything?

GEORGE. Remember Honor. I *have* worked hard.

Beat.

HONOR. What does that mean?

GEORGE. That's all. That's all.

HONOR. And *I* haven't?

GEORGE. Of course. Of course. And Gerry will look after you.

HONOR. Even I know we can't have the same lawyer, George. We can't both have *our* lawyer –

GEORGE. You have Gerry. That's what I'm saying. That's what I'm saying. I'll look after myself.

HONOR. *Yes.*

GEORGE. I'll find someone.

HONOR. What do you think our lawyers will resolve, George?

GEORGE (*embarrassed*). The – the houses – you know – The shares.

HONOR. The houses?

GEORGE. Yes.

HONOR. If you want the houses, George, you can have them.

GEORGE. No! No! That's the point! You need to be *practical*, Honor. I want you to be comfortable.

HONOR. Comfortable?

GEORGE. Obviously, neither of us is going to be able to live extravagantly. I can't support two – two households.

HONOR. Two households?

GEORGE. Even I am a household, Honor. Even I am a household.

HONOR. What will I – Where will I – ? (*Realising.*) How will I live?

GEORGE. Honor, you'll be all right. I promise. You'll be allright.

HONOR. You *promise*?

GEORGE. Yes.

HONOR (*angry*). And what does that mean? What does that mean when you promise something? That I'll be alright for some time? That I'll get used to things being alright? That I'll feel comfortable and safe? And then, and then when you feel like it – When you feel like making a change –

GEORGE. I'll call Gerry and tell him what's going on and we'll have a meeting – You're not – You're not destitute, Honor. If you're careful, you'll – I'm sure you'll manage.

HONOR. We're dividing *everything*, are we?

GEORGE. I suppose so.

HONOR. So let's – I tell you what – Let's divide the misery too. And the joy! The joy! *You* take half my misery and *I'll* take half your new found joy.

Scene Fourteen

CLAUDIA. I'd use the word –

GEORGE. Obnoxious.

CLAUDIA. No. No.

GEORGE. Loud.

CLAUDIA. 'Cutting edge', actually –

GEORGE. Three words –

CLAUDIA. Very 'now'. You should –

GEORGE. It's not my –

CLAUDIA. Be open! Be open –

GEORGE. I'm reviewing – I have half a book to finish –

CLAUDIA. You said to me – You said to me – You *promised* –

GEORGE. Next time. Darling. Darling one. Next time I'll go
    and see – Dead Sock or Bitch Dog or whatever they're –

CLAUDIA. Fine. (*Beat.*) Fine.

He looks at her tenderly.

GEORGE. My girl. My own girl.

CLAUDIA (*she has forgiven him*). Who's the review for?

GEORGE. Bernie Woodman. The Quarterly.

CLAUDIA. He's still editing?

GEORGE. Yes.

CLAUDIA. He's a friend?

GEORGE. Bernie and I go back – He's an old friend –

CLAUDIA. I'd like to meet him –

GEORGE. You'd like him –

CLAUDIA. I'd like to meet him –

GEORGE. Sure!

CLAUDIA. We could have a – we could – have lunch, maybe?

GEORGE (*casually*). Sure!

CLAUDIA. Next weekend?

GEORGE. If you like.

Beat.

CLAUDIA (*tentatively*). Did you – read . . . ?

GEORGE (*uncomfortable but semi-expecting it*). Yes. Yes
   I did.

Beat.

CLAUDIA. And?

GEORGE *pauses.*

GEORGE (*searching*). Some *terrific* stuff there. (*Beat.*) It had
   a – *lovely* – There was a quality to the writing that was –
   that was – very, very – nice.

CLAUDIA. Nice?

GEORGE. *Very* nice. And some great – really great moments –
   When she's talking to the guy in the club! Great! (*Quietly.*)
   Great . . .

CLAUDIA. There's an irony there –

GEORGE. Exactly. Exactly.

CLAUDIA. Which works, I think –

GEORGE. *Absolutely.* The irony – it's really . . . beautifully –
   ironic. I love that.

CLAUDIA. You do?

GEORGE. I love it.

CLAUDIA. I thought I'd submit it . . .

GEORGE (*a little surprised*). Aha –

CLAUDIA (*alerted*). What?

GEORGE. Of course you could. Sure! Why not?

CLAUDIA. But I sense – I sense – You don't think I –

GEORGE. If you feel – Of course you're – It's your decision –

CLAUDIA. But *you* don't think –

GEORGE. Well, it might – I don't want you to – It can take quite a few rejection slips before –

CLAUDIA. Rejection – ? You think –

GEORGE. No! No. I don't *think* – But it's – It's a very subjective business.

CLAUDIA. You're saying – ?

GEORGE. It might be worth – staying with it . . .

CLAUDIA. It's not – ? What? What's wrong?

GEORGE. Not 'wrong'. Not wrong.

CLAUDIA. Well? Well?

GEORGE. There's a –

CLAUDIA. Yes – Yes –

GEORGE. A touch of –

CLAUDIA. Of what?

GEORGE. I'm – (*Backing off.*) I'm not sure I can put my finger –

CLAUDIA. George! Come *on*!

GEORGE. Well, a certain – In the characterisation – a certain –

CLAUDIA. What? *Say* it!

GEORGE. Sometimes you go just a little too – directly – to the gist of a character – There's a kind of – over-clarity . . .

CLAUDIA. 'Over-clarity'?

GEORGE. A kind of –

CLAUDIA. You're saying –

GEORGE. A directness.

CLAUDIA. An obviousness? (*Taking it in.*) An *obviousness*?

GEORGE. Too strong! – Oh no! – *No*!

CLAUDIA. An obviousness.

GEORGE. You're being much too hard on your – *No*. It's about – (*Beat.*) – *nuance*.

CLAUDIA. Nuance?

Beat.

You know, you're very –

GEORGE. What?

CLAUDIA. Locked in.

GEORGE. Locked? What?

CLAUDIA. A certain view. A certain way of –

GEORGE. Of *course* I am!

CLAUDIA. It's inevitable. A generational thing.

GEORGE. I see . . .

CLAUDIA. A way of. Writing has – It's – Style, you know. It's – There are things happening.

GEORGE. That's true.

CLAUDIA. You may not be – Your opinion is not the –

GEORGE. Absolutely. And you're – You're going to be a good writer. Of course you are. And you're so – beautiful. You're my – You're my – (*Beat.*) Come to me.

Scene Fifteen

HONOR (*with playful confidence*). The Far East.

GEORGE. The Far East?

HONOR. Let's talk about it.

GEORGE. What?

HONOR. I've been thinking –

GEORGE. What?

HONOR. Let's get rid of the pension fund.

GEORGE. *What*?

HONOR. Reinvest in the Far East. It's looking promising again . . .

Beat.

Let's sell the house in France – it's a tiny return, and stick half in Abbey National – split the dividends, then reinvest if we're feeling frisky in twelve months –

GEORGE. I can't believe –

HONOR. There's some interesting property opportunities in Spain . . .

GEORGE. Don't be ridiculous!

HONOR. Could be risky, but then you only live once. (*Beat.*) Or twice . . .

GEORGE. This isn't *you*.

HONOR. Why shouldn't it be?

GEORGE. Because it just *isn't*.

HONOR. I'm taking your advice, George. I'm being practical.

GEORGE. I look after the investments – That's my – *I* do that.

HONOR. Well, no. No, George. I rather think I should like to do it.

GEORGE. You don't – Honor, for Christ's sake. This is our future. You've never been – You've never been interested in money.

HONOR. And you've never been interested in adultery. Isn't change a thrill? (*Beat.*) You know, I realise now that you were right, in a way. That distance makes you rethink and in that space, new truth comes through. What I love, what I loved, was the knowing of what the next day carried to me, the sweet certainties which belong to a shared life. You think it's inane to love order but order was my freedom. Do I love you, George? Perhaps I loved *belonging* to you – and thus to the earth, in fact, to the very earth?

GEORGE. What do you want from me?

HONOR. I want to make you feel a memory of this. So that one day in a fleeting moment, you feel the surest sense of lovelessness and through that – the unmistakable clasp of terror.

Scene Sixteen

CLAUDIA. He doesn't know.

HONOR. He doesn't.

CLAUDIA. Know. I'm here.

HONOR. I'm busy.

CLAUDIA. Yes.

Beat.

The first time I came here, I – I remember the books – so many books – (*Beat.*) We didn't have many books. My parents weren't – great – readers – (*Beat.*) If I have a child, I will – I'm going to read to them and buy them books . . .

HONOR. Sophie liked books when she was very young. We read to her a lot.

CLAUDIA. Sometimes I look at – well, doing this book, you enter people's houses, you glimpse the things they take as normal, you get a sense of how life is for them and I – sometimes I see how – Your daughter – how lucky she is . . .

HONOR. Sophie?

CLAUDIA. To have so much – to have such a solid – (*Beat.*) I longed for parents like you.

HONOR. Like us?

CLAUDIA. Bookish. Clever. Idealistic. I invented you. I dreamt you up. I knew you before I even met you, Honor – I glimpsed the future.

HONOR. I always used to see the future as devastation and when it came, it melted into the ordinary present. I began to see that my fear was just a campaign to camouflage my relentless good fortune. What fabulous irony! That just as I begin to lose my appetite for imagining catastrophe, catastrophe actually happens.

CLAUDIA. Do you still love – are you – are you still . . . ?

HONOR. I don't know.

CLAUDIA. I've been thinking about – I've been thinking –

HONOR. No.

CLAUDIA. Please –

HONOR. Don't let me in on this – Don't make me watch you grow up.

CLAUDIA. I thought you'd want –

HONOR. No. (*Pause.*) No.

CLAUDIA. You should know –

HONOR. Everything is different. Things don't change and then change back. Whatever happens. I'm – I'm – To tell

you the truth, I've barely begun to understand it. I'm
writing. I'm living. I'm surviving. They're all good things,
I suppose. If I could go back – I would go back. I don't like
travel of any kind. But that's – beside – Look Claudia, you
get on with what you need to do. You live your life the way
you need to. You form your ideas. You go to extremes. You
learn your lessons. You come to regret. That may be your
story. But I'm not interested. I only know that once I was
two and now I am one. Maybe that's a good thing, in the
end. But whether or not it is, it's happened.

Beat.

CLAUDIA. Will you forgive me?

HONOR. I'm trying to see you as just a baby, just a tiny baby
with that sweet pulse in your soft skull, and clear naked
skin – I'm trying so hard to see you there, loved, loving,
new. And that makes me feel – That makes me feel –
Perhaps . . .

CLAUDIA. I wish I could write like you.

HONOR. Good.

Scene Seventeen

CLAUDIA (*agitated, distressed*). Why does the heart take
precedence?

GEORGE. Why does the heart?

CLAUDIA. Yes. Yes, I mean. I'm asking you. Why does the
heart take precedence?

GEORGE. Over – over what?

CLAUDIA. You're asking me?

GEORGE. Over what?

CLAUDIA. You're asking me?

GEORGE. Yes –

CLAUDIA. Over kindness. Over loyalty. Over history. Whatever. Let's say: Justice.

GEORGE. Justice.

CLAUDIA. Yes.

GEORGE. I can't believe you're asking me!

CLAUDIA. Why shouldn't I?

GEORGE. Because the heart, the heart *in this case*, the heart which is 'taking precedence' is taking it in, in your direction.

CLAUDIA. And that means I can't ask you whether that's a good thing?

GEORGE. The heart is choosing – Is choosing *you*. It's choosing *you*.

CLAUDIA. Tell me why the heart wins.

GEORGE. Why the heart wins?

CLAUDIA. Yes.

GEORGE. Why wouldn't it win?

CLAUDIA. When we see a – a gold ring on someone's hand and we want it, we don't take it do we? We don't mug them do we?

GEORGE. Loving you. Loving you – you see this as – as mugging Honor? *You*?

CLAUDIA. We don't take it because – It's unlawful wanting, isn't it?

Silence.

But when we want someone, we call that – we call that loving . . .

GEORGE. Yes –

CLAUDIA. Even when – even when others may be – may be –

GEORGE. That's. That's simplistic. That's childish!

CLAUDIA. That's unlawful loving, isn't it?

GEORGE. You're asking me this?

CLAUDIA. And yet because it's the heart, somehow, somehow, some sense of poetry creeps in as if, as if – as if the heart has no judges –

GEORGE. The heart is the truth. If you ignore it – if you ignore it – what then? What life is that? For all of us? If I go back and live the life I lead, knowing this – my darling, my darling – what then?

CLAUDIA. What then?

GEORGE. Do you think that's better for her?

Beat.

CLAUDIA. Maybe –

GEORGE. For me?

CLAUDIA. Maybe that too. Because when all the fuss has died down, when it doesn't give you that thrill, that thrill to see me waiting for you in the theatre foyer, in my short skirt, then – then you might start to think: What Have I Done?

GEORGE. You say that as if you think I've done wrong.

CLAUDIA. And you might not *like* the answer. In the cold light –

GEORGE. In the cold light I will know that I did the only thing that I could do.

CLAUDIA. But thousands don't, do they?

GEORGE. Don't –

CLAUDIA. They don't throw out –

GEORGE. Jesus!

CLAUDIA. Throw out their wives. They sit there inside secret lives, they nurse their untaken steps because – because –

GEORGE. Of cowardice –

CLAUDIA. And sometimes – another – another kind of love –

GEORGE. Another love?

CLAUDIA. A love of – of fairness – or even – a love for themselves as they want to be. True.

GEORGE. True but not truth-full.

CLAUDIA. You see this as the truth, George. You and me.

GEORGE. Yes.

CLAUDIA. But she is the truth too.

Beat.

And what if the truth is that we do not know love because we do not know how to deny ourselves anything?

Beat.

GEORGE (*incredulous*). Don't know how to – to – My God, what does it – what does it *take*? I haven't denied myself anything? Only my *life*! Only my, my – Do you think I never stop to think – all of it, thirty –

CLAUDIA. Thirty-two. (*Beat.*) Did I ask you?

GEORGE. No – No.

CLAUDIA. I remember, I remember very clearly saying I demand nothing from you, you are your own –

GEORGE. Agent, yes.

CLAUDIA. Yes. Agent.

GEORGE. I regret nothing. Nothing, my darling. Nothing. But don't you think, don't you think, I *feel* what has been lost?

CLAUDIA. Well, then –

GEORGE. What are the pleasures of getting old, if not to know oneself and the fixtures around you? To have the blessings of intimacy? I wake up and know how I relate to my bed, to my work, to my wife, to the night, to the universe,

in fact. My body marching into it, moving towards the
darkness, the space, the dust, the dust . . . I have a tally of
my ambitions: my rates of success, my sorrows, all I once
hoped for, all that has been met, and all that I now know
I can never be. The cleverness that never amounted to genius.
The kindness that never amounted to saintliness. The wit
which touched charisma but in the end, failed to claim it.
What greater comfort can there be than the certainty of
knowing what you have become and what you belong to . . .

CLAUDIA. Or who.

GEORGE. Or who. (*Beat.*) I've given everything away to love
you.

CLAUDIA. Yes. Everything. Maybe. Maybe you have.

Silence. Stillness in her. She turns to him.

Why *am* I so certain?

GEORGE. About?

CLAUDIA. Everything.

GEORGE. Why are you so certain?

CLAUDIA. Is it knowledge, George – or is it – or is it – fear?
I wanted you –

GEORGE. You have me –

CLAUDIA. I wanted you to love me –

GEORGE. I love you –

CLAUDIA. I call for you –

GEORGE. I answer you –

CLAUDIA. And the smaller that gap between our voices, the
stronger, the sweeter I feel, as if all the realness is – is
smothered in us – there is only us –

GEORGE. There *is* only us –

CLAUDIA. And Honor!

GEORGE. Honor's gone!

CLAUDIA. At night I feel her fingers in the darkness, creeping over me.

GEORGE. Forget Honor!

CLAUDIA. As if – as if – she knows me – will not let me go –

GEORGE. Forget Honor. Christ! It's us now!

CLAUDIA. How wondrous it is to let yourself be – be – at a loss, alone . . .

GEORGE. You're telling me you admire my wife?

CLAUDIA. I look at myself and I think why is my voice so clear? Why do my words sound so satisfied with themselves?

GEORGE. What?

CLAUDIA. Can anyone that sure of themself feel anything?

GEORGE. You feel things!

CLAUDIA. When you read my work –

GEORGE. That's – that's different!

CLAUDIA. You felt then – You saw –

GEORGE. You feel things!

CLAUDIA. Do I? Do I?

GEORGE. We feel things!

CLAUDIA. Do you George? Or are you like me? Choosing a life, answering every mystery with a certainty, composing ourselves through each other. Is there any – any grace here? When there is no doubt. Is there the *grace* to love?

GEORGE. Are you saying –

CLAUDIA. What loss is within me?

GEORGE. What? What?

CLAUDIA. Honor. Asked me. She said to me: What loss is within you?

GEORGE. She's cast a spell – she's manipulating you!

CLAUDIA. She was – showing me – she was – (*Beat.*) There is nothing here, George – Here (*Indicating her heart.*)

GEORGE. You don't love me?

CLAUDIA. I love – (*Beat.*) – To be loved . . .

GEORGE. You don't love me?

CLAUDIA. When you touch me, it's as if my body falls into place . . .

GEORGE. And that's not love?

CLAUDIA. And when you speak to me – that way – that way that you do – When you tell me things – I feel – I feel – as if I am in a story, and it wraps around me, because because I'm important to you . . .

GEORGE. You *are* important to me!

CLAUDIA. And you'll want to make me happy and part of you. That when I call for you –

GEORGE. I'll listen.

CLAUDIA. And that my loss will –

GEORGE. Devastate me –

CLAUDIA. That my loss will –

GEORGE. Devastate me.

CLAUDIA. And that my loss will . . .

They look at each other.

Silence. The truth is suddenly felt by both of them.

GEORGE. That is what love is to you – ?

CLAUDIA. To know that –

GEORGE. Yes . . . ?

CLAUDIA. I can undo you.

GEORGE. That's how you love me?

CLAUDIA. I'm sorry.

GEORGE. Yes.

CLAUDIA. I'm so sorry . . .

Scene Eighteen

HONOR. She said to me – she said 'It's just a piece of paper'.

GEORGE. That's Sophie.

HONOR. She didn't want us to come – She said it was 'irrelevant' – I told her we were proud –

GEORGE. Yes –

HONOR. Our little girl.

GEORGE. Of course if she worked a little harder –

HONOR. Well –

GEORGE. She never fulfilled her – She could have done better . . .

Beat.

Thanks for sending me –

HONOR. You got it –

GEORGE. I liked it. Very much. (*Beat.*) You didn't inscribe it.

HONOR. No.

GEORGE. I found it . . .

HONOR. Well . . .

GEORGE. Hard to read. (*Beat.*) It was good work.

Beat.

The reviews – they were –

HONOR. Yes. That was. I think they recognised a certain –

GEORGE. Yes –

HONOR. A certain –

GEORGE. Yes –

HONOR. Truth.

Beat.

GEORGE. You know – it's funny – one thing –

HONOR. No.

GEORGE. One thing –

HONOR. No.

GEORGE. I dream of us. (*Beat.*) A time before.

Beat.

And there –

HONOR. There –

GEORGE. In sleep –

HONOR. Yes –

GEORGE. Is the only place I feel – Complete.

Beat.

HONOR. It's too –

GEORGE. I know.

HONOR. It's too –

GEORGE. I know.

HONOR. It's –

Blackout.

End.